Original title:
Crafting Creative Narratives

Copyright © 2024 Book Fairy Publishing
All rights reserved.

Author: Melani Helimets
ISBN HARDBACK: 978-9916-87-726-5
ISBN PAPERBACK: 978-9916-87-727-2
ISBN EBOOK: 978-9916-87-728-9

## Mythos in Motion

In the dawn where dreams arise,
Legends dance beneath the skies.
Whispers weave through the soft air,
Echoes of hopes beyond compare.

Every step a story told,
With hearts of fire, brave and bold.
The past ignites the present's light,
As shadows turn to endless bright.

## The Resonance of Voices

In the chorus of the free,
Voices rise like waves at sea.
Each note a thread of shared delight,
Binding souls in the soft twilight.

Harmony that soothes the soul,
Together we can feel whole.
With every word, a heart will sing,
In unity, we find our wings.

## Vignettes of the Vivid

Painted dreams in vibrant hues,
Brushstrokes of passion in the blues.
Moments captured in flowing grace,
Life unfolds in a timeless space.

Each vignette a treasure true,
In the tapestry, me and you.
Through our eyes, the world will spin,
In every loss, a chance to win.

## Woven Whimsies

Starlit nights where dreams entwine,
Woven whimsies, life's design.
Imagination's playful breeze,
Lifts the spirits, sets them free.

Laughter lingers, soft and sweet,
In every moment, life's heartbeat.
With open hearts, we leap and soar,
Finding magic at every door.

## The Art of the Untamed Pen

With ink that flows like rivers wide,
Ideas dance, and dreams collide.
Each stroke a whisper, bold and free,
A world unfolds for you to see.

Unchained spirit, wild and true,
The pen ignites what's deep in you.
Rough edges shaped by heart's embrace,
Create your path, your sacred space.

In shadows cast and light revealed,
The stories birth, their truth unsealed.
With every word, the soul takes flight,
Transforming darkness into light.

Let passion guide as you explore,
The canvas wide, your spirit soar.
With courage found in every line,
The art you make is truly divine.

So take the time, unleash your voice,
In the wild journey, make your choice.
With every heartbeat, with every pen,
Create a tale, let it begin.

## Luminous Fables

In twilight's glow, the stories bloom,
Each fable casts away the gloom.
With every turn of luminous page,
A brighter world, a vibrant stage.

Whispers of wisdom, soft and clear,
Through woven tales, the soul draws near.
Adventures spun from pure delight,
In hearts ignited, sparks of light.

From heroes bold to gentle dreams,
The thread of magic softly gleams.
With courage found in tales of old,
The future shines; let dreams unfold.

A tapestry of joy and strife,
In fables told, we find our life.
Invite the wonder, embrace the new,
Let luminous tales empower you.

So read aloud and share the spark,
In every story, make your mark.
For each fable, shared and cherished,
Keeps hope alive, and fears perish.

# **Textures of Thought**

Through layers deep, the mind explores,
In textured realms, imagination soars.
Each thought a thread, rich and profound,
In tapestry woven, meaning's found.

With colors bright and shadows dark,
The landscape twists, igniting spark.
Ideas meld like clay in hands,
Creating worlds where vision stands.

Feel every nuance, embrace the flow,
Let curiosity guide you to grow.
In the fabric of dreams, find your way,
As textures of thought paint your day.

In quiet moments, wisdom flows,
As gentle breezes through the rose.
The dance of ideas, fluid and free,
Invites the whispers of possibility.

So seek the depths, uncover each part,
For in your mind, lies boundless art.
Create with courage, unafraid to feel,
In textures of thought, your truth is real.

## Sketches of the Soul

With charcoal dreams upon the page,
Sketches form that transcend the age.
In gentle strokes, emotions blend,
The soul's great journey, a timeless friend.

Each line a pulse, each curve a sigh,
Unfolding visions as clouds drift by.
With every mark, a story told,
In each creation, the heart unfolds.

In colors bright, or shades of gray,
The inner light finds its own way.
Through artful whispers, feelings rise,
Revealing truths beneath the skies.

So take your time, let canvases breathe,
In sketches made, dreamers believe.
For every stroke can heal the pain,
Drawing hope from loss, like summer rain.

Embrace the art that lives inside,
With every sketch, let beauty guide.
For in those lines, the spirit sings,
Creating wonders that passion brings.

## **The Story Weavers' Dance**

In twilight's glow, hands intertwine,
Weaving tales that brightly shine.
Each thread a wish, a spark of hope,
Together we rise, learn to cope.

With every step, the rhythm flows,
The heart recalls what wisdom knows.
We dance as one, a sacred art,
Creating futures that won't depart.

Lifted by dreams, the spirit soars,
Opening wide the timeless doors.
With laughter's light, we chase the sun,
In the dance of life, we are all one.

Embrace the night, let stars ignite,
Our voices blend in pure delight.
Together we write a vibrant fate,
In unity strong, we celebrate.

Each story told, a fire anew,
In the tapestry, me and you.
We are the weavers, watch us spin,
The dance of life, where we begin.

## Echoes of the Untold

In whispers soft, the echoes call,
Unwritten tales of rise and fall.
Each heartbeat holds a secret song,
Reminding us where we belong.

Through valleys deep and mountains high,
Our dreams take flight, they learn to fly.
With every challenge that we face,
We find the strength, we find our grace.

History lives in shadows vast,
But hope will rise, it's built to last.
The courage found within the night,
Transforms the dark into pure light.

With open minds, we chart the course,
Each untold dream, a hidden force.
Together we carve a destiny,
In unity, we'll always be.

Let voices blend, let spirits soar,
Unlock the locks, reveal the door.
Echoes speak, and we will hear,
The stories whispered, ever near.

## **Shadows of a Distant Dream**

Through misty paths, our visions gleam,
In the heart of hope lies a distant dream.
We chase the shadows, find our way,
Painting the night, igniting the day.

Each moment counts, let's not delay,
With every breath, we pave the way.
The glow of courage lights the dark,
Filling our souls with a passionate spark.

Our dreams may fade, yet still they call,
Inspire the brave to stand up tall.
With strength united against the tide,
We hold the future, arms open wide.

Through trials faced, our spirits rise,
Transforming fears into the skies.
The distant dream is now so near,
Together, we conquer every fear.

With open hearts and minds so free,
We shape the world, our own decree.
In shadows cast, our light will beam,
Together we weave the distant dream.

# Pages Unwritten

Upon the page, the pen awaits,
To carve our truths and shift the fates.
Each line a heartbeat, each stroke a wish,
Crafting magic, fulfilling bliss.

The ink flows bright with colors bold,
As stories unbound begin to unfold.
With every chapter, we dare to dream,
Creating realities, a flowing stream.

The tales of old guide us on,
Yet we'll ignite the light of dawn.
In unexplored lands, we take the leap,
Awakening dreams that wake us from sleep.

Turn the page—a new adventure awaits,
In every choice, destiny creates.
Together we'll write our legacy,
Inherent power, forever free.

So grasp the pen, let stories flow,
In harmony, let our spirits grow.
Each page unwritten, a chance to start,
Crafting the future, with love at heart.

# The Heart's Narrative

In quiet whispers, dreams take flight,
Through shadows creeping, they seek the light.
Each heartbeat carries tales untold,
With courage ignited, we become bold.

In every challenge, a lesson lies,
Beneath dark clouds, an endless sky.
Hope is a journey, not a race,
In the heart's narrative, find your place.

With every stumble, growth will bloom,
In the aftermath, dispel the gloom.
A tapestry woven, bright and wide,
In unity and love, we will abide.

We rise as one, through storm and strife,
The heart's anthem, a song of life.
With every heartbeat, we stand tall,
Together we flourish, together we call.

Embrace the journey, paint it bright,
With every color, we chase the light.
In the heart's narrative, we are free,
Unfolding stories, for all to see.

## **Altar of Stories**

Gather 'round the altar of tales,
In every heartbeat, a voice prevails.
History whispers in the quiet night,
Each story a spark, igniting the light.

In the tapestry woven from threads of gold,
Wisdom is shared, and dreams unfold.
Each tale a beacon, shining so bright,
Guiding the lost through the darkest night.

From ashes of sorrow, hope takes flight,
Resilience blooms, even in blight.
Together we stand, hand in hand,
With love as our compass, we will expand.

Every heart beats with courage deep,
In the altar of stories, we dare to leap.
With every breath, we write our song,
In unity and strength, we all belong.

So gather 'round with open hearts,
In this sacred circle, no one departs.
Each voice a treasure, each moment divine,
In the altar of stories, let us shine.

## Fables from Forgotten Times

In pages worn, the fables call,
Echoes of wisdom in shadows fall.
Stories of courage, and love so true,
From forgotten times, they guide us through.

With every tale, a lesson blooms,
In ancient whispers, the spirit resumes.
Through trials endured, and triumphs gained,
The heart's resolve is beautifully strained.

A phoenix rising, from ashes we grow,
In the fables told, the truth will flow.
Bridges we build from past to now,
With every story, we make a vow.

To honor the voices that came before,
In the fables of time, we find our core.
Each heart a chapter, each life a rhyme,
In the dance of existence, we transcend time.

So gather the tales, let them ignite,
In the heart of the world, we find our light.
In fables from ages, forever entwined,
The spark of connection, the thread that binds.

## Voices in the Margins

In whispers soft, the unheard sing,
Voices in the margins, hope they bring.
Through trials faced, their spirits soar,
In quiet strength, we find the core.

With stories rich, they carve the way,
In shadows deep, they find the day.
Every heartbeat a testament true,
In the margins' embrace, we find our crew.

Together we rise, unyielding and bold,
In unity's warmth, let the truth be told.
From the edges of silence, courage loud,
The voices we cherish, together we're proud.

Through all the struggles, through every test,
In the margins' embrace, we find our rest.
Every story shared is a step in grace,
In the voices' chorus, we find our place.

So listen closely, let your heart ignite,
In the margins' wisdom, reveal the light.
Together we journey, hand in hand,
With voices united, together we stand.

## The Alchemy of Words

Words are like seeds, they grow
In hearts where hope is sown.
Each letter a spark, a light,
Igniting dreams, taking flight.

In whispers soft, the tales begin,
With courage found from deep within.
They weave a spell, a vibrant hue,
Transforming thoughts, making them new.

With every pen stroke, magic flows,
Empowering souls, where wisdom grows.
They craft a symphony of the mind,
A treasure trove for all mankind.

Through pages worn, journeys unfold,
In every story, a truth retold.
They challenge fate, they break the mold,
In the realm of words, we are bold.

Let your voice be a guiding star,
No matter how lost, you'll never be far.
For in this alchemy of light,
We find our way, through day and night.

## **Forging Fantasies**

In the forge of dreams, we stand,
Crafting visions with heart and hand.
Every wish, a glowing fire,
Fueling hopes that never tire.

The hammer strikes, each beat, a goal,
Shaping desires deep in the soul.
With every spark, our spirits rise,
Creating worlds behind our eyes.

Imagination's strength is true,
In colors bright, we chase the blue.
With passion fierce, we carve our fate,
With fantasies that celebrate.

Through trials faced, each lesson learned,\nIn the heat of dreams, our hearts have burned.
Emerging strong from shadows cast,
In the forge of life, connection lasts.

So let us dare to chase the light,
For in these dreams, we find our flight.
Embrace the magic that we hold,
And brand our tales in threads of gold.

# Inked Journeys

With ink-stained hands, we write our paths,
Charting courses through joy and wrath.
Each sentence a step, a leap to take,
With every word, new roads we make.

In the quiet place where thoughts collide,
Stories form, like waves, we ride.
Through valleys low and mountains high,
Our inked journeys will never die.

Letters dance upon the page,
Capturing youth, wisdom, and age.
They whisper secrets, dreams untold,
In every tale, a vision bold.

We sail through realms with ink as our guide,
Each verse a compass, our hearts the tide.
In the book of life, where hopes reside,
Every chapter, a journey wide.

So let us write with hearts ablaze,
Inked journeys through the endless haze.
For every page turned is a start,
A canvas painted with the heart.

## The Tapestry of Tales

Threads of stories, woven tight,
In colors rich, they bring delight.
Each tale a strand, unique yet whole,
Weaving together, heart and soul.

From whispers soft to loud refrains,
The tapestry grows, as joy remains.
In every knot, a lesson learned,
In every pattern, love discerned.

Through laughter shared and sorrows bared,\nIn
this tapestry, we all have cared.
Our tales entwined with destiny's thread,
In the fabric of time, where dreams are fed.

With every twist, a new surprise,
In the art of stories, wisdom lies.
Together we stand, in unity's grace,
As we stitch our lives, in this sacred space.

So let us weave with hearts wide open,
For every thread speaks words unspoken.
In the grand design, we find our place,
In the tapestry of tales, we embrace.

## Chronicles of the Untold

In shadows where the silence grows,
Dreams linger like untold prose.
Each heartbeat hums a secret song,
A melody where we belong.

Beneath the stars, weaving fate,
In every pulse, a chance awaits.
With every step, the journey calls,
In the depths, we rise, we fall.

Through valleys deep, our spirits soar,
With whispers of the ones before.
Holding tight to hope's embrace,
We venture forth, we find our place.

With pen in hand, we write our tale,
Against the odds, we shall not fail.
These chronicles of heart and mind,
Unfolding truths we seek to find.

A spark ignites, a world revealed,
The strength within, forever healed.
We chart the paths we yet to roam,
In unity, we create our home.

## Sketching the Invisible

With strokes of thought, our dreams take flight,
Imagining worlds hidden from sight.
A canvas blank, our hearts await,
To fill the space, the hands of fate.

In shades of hope, we find our tone,
The colors blend, and we are known.
Each line a promise, soft yet bold,
A vision of the dreams we've told.

As shadows dance and light awakes,
We paint our truths, no fear, no breaks.
With every mark, the whispers grow,
An unseen depth, our spirits show.

In every breath, we sketch the dawn,
The beauty found in the reborn.
These images, forever bright,
In our hearts, they hold the light.

Through artistry, we dare to dream,
In every heartbeat, hope will gleam.
With brushes dry, yet spirits wet,
We sketch the world we won't forget.

## Prose in Motion

In time's embrace, we walk as one,
With every word, new journeys spun.
The tales we craft, they dance and play,
A testament to dreams by day.

As rivers flow, our stories drift,
In every heart, a precious gift.
The silence speaks, in whispers clear,
With prose in motion, we conquer fear.

Each moment penned, a legacy,
In ink and spirit, we are free.
Together, we traverse the lines,
Creating worlds where hope aligns.

Through laughter's grace and sorrow's tears,
We write our truth through all the years.
In every passage, we embrace,
The nuances of the human race.

With every story, we ignite,
A flame of will, a beacon light.
In prose we grow, in words we shine,
A tapestry of souls entwined.

## The Cartographer of Dreams

In maps unseen, our visions grow,
A cartographer, we trace, we sow.
Each thought, a compass, guides our way,
Towards horizons, new dawns play.

With ink and star, we draw the skies,
In every glance, a new surprise.
The dreams we harbor, bold and wild,
With every heartbeat, we are styled.

Through valleys low and mountains high,
We chart the course where eagles fly.
The lands unknown, so vast, so grand,
A journey led by heart and hand.

In every step, the future calls,
With faith in hand, we shatter walls.
For every dream that yearns, awaits,
A world alive, where hope creates.

In canvas made of endless skies,
We sketch the dreams, and watch them rise.
A cartographer of hopes untold,
In every heart, a map of gold.

## The World Beneath the Words

In silence whispers dreams unfold,
Boundless stories yet untold.
With every sentence, faith ignites,
Guiding souls to hidden lights.

The pages turn, the heart believes,
In every line, the spirit weaves.
Hope is forged in ink and space,
A timeless dance, a warm embrace.

The echoes of the past resound,
In written lines, our truth is found.
From paper's grasp, we learn to soar,
The world awaits, it's ours to explore.

When shadows fall and doubts arise,
Look to the words, they are the prize.
For in them dwell our greatest fears,
And all the dreams that conquer years.

Let pens become the swords we wield,
And every truth a shining shield.
Together in this sacred space,
We'll find the strength to run the race.

# Fragmented Fancies

A puzzle pieced with dreams so bright,
In colors bold, they spark delight.
Each fragment whispers, secrets shared,
In scattered thoughts, our hearts laid bare.

The mind, a canvas, paints the skies,
Where wishes bloom and courage lies.
With every stroke, a vision grows,
Like sunlight kissing winter's snows.

We gather dreams like fallen leaves,
In vibrant hues, the heart believes.
Caught in the breeze of hope's embrace,
Each moment shines, a warm grace.

The journey flows, a river wild,
In every heart, a caring child.
With laughter bright and spirits high,
We'll learn to dance and touch the sky.

So chase the fancies, let hearts sing,
In tangled webs, new joy they bring.
For life is but a tapestry,
Woven with threads of destiny.

## **Silken Threads of Thoughts**

In gentle whispers, thoughts take flight,
With every thread, we weave the light.
From heart to mind, a silk-like flow,
Creating paths where dreams can grow.

The fabric of our lives, so bright,
Is stitched with care, a wondrous sight.
In every color, stories blend,
A tapestry that will not end.

With passion's fire, we ignite the day,
As visions dance, and shadows play.
Each moment captured, held so dear,
In silken threads, we banish fear.

So trace the lines, let spirits soar,
With courage deep and hearts that roar.
For in this web, we find our way,
An endless dream that bodes the day.

Weaving kindness, hope, and grace,
Through every challenge that we face.
For life's a thread, so strong and fine,
Embrace the art; let our hearts shine.

# Unfolding Enigmas

In mysteries that lie awake,
We search for paths that dreams can make.
Each question asked, a world revealed,
In riddles deep, our fate is sealed.

The journey whispers truths concealed,
With each new answer, joy is healed.
As stars align and shadows fade,
The unknown beckons, unafraid.

In winding ways, our spirits glide,
Through every twist, we learn to ride.
With open hearts, we chase the light,
Embracing all that feels so right.

In darkest nights, our dreams ignite,
A spark within, a guiding light.
Together here, we break the chains,
And dance through life, as love remains.

So trust the path that lies ahead,
In every step, new hope is fed.
For life's a puzzle, vast, profound,
Unfolding secrets, joy unbound.

# The Symphony of Sentences

In the quiet moments, words align,
Creating harmony, a soul's design.
With every whisper, a story grows,
A melody of life, as wisdom flows.

Through pages turned, the heart takes flight,
In tales of courage, we find our light.
The ink dances across the page,
Inspiring dreams that never age.

Each sentence crafted with tender care,
Resonates deep, a song laid bare.
Together we rise, hand in hand,
In the symphony of sentences, we stand.

Let hope be the drum that guides our way,
A rhythm of joy in each new day.
As we write our fate with no regrets,
In unity, our essence reflects.

So lift your voice, let your spirit soar,
In every heartbeat, hear the roar.
For in this symphony, we find our place,
A celebration of life, and love's embrace.

## Melodies of the Mind

In the depths of thought, a song emerges,
Wisdom flows where imagination surges.
Each note a vision, vibrant and clear,
A landscape of dreams, drawing us near.

With every echo, possibilities unfold,
Stories of triumph in whispers told.
The rhythm of hope, steady and bright,
Guiding us kindly through darkest night.

Dance with the verses, sway with the tune,
A ballet of passions beneath the moon.
Unlock the wonders, let the heart see,
In melodies of the mind, we are free.

Embrace the silence, let it resonate,
The beauty of thoughts, a wondrous state.
Notes intertwine, creating a spell,
In the music of dreams, we all can dwell.

As we journey onward, tune into grace,
In this grand orchestra, find your place.
For life is a melody, endless and bold,
A symphony waiting, ready to unfold.

# Labyrinths of Meaning

In the maze of thought, we seek the path,
Each twist and turn ignites the mind's wrath.
Yet through the shadows, wisdom will shine,
Revealing the beauty of the vine.

Every question posed, a doorway swings,
Unlocking the potential that knowledge brings.
In labyrinths deep, we wander and roam,
Finding our way to a place called home.

With every answer, a new door appears,
Connecting the dots, dissolving our fears.
The journey is rich, so vast and profound,
In the dance of discovery, truth is found.

In the whispers of meaning, we forge our way,
Building a bridge for a brighter day.
For within the chaos, clarity awaits,
In the labyrinth of life, open the gates.

So embrace the journey, and welcome the quest,
For every trial is a chance to invest.
In the heart of the maze, let passion ignite,
And find your own path to the limitless light.

## **Ink Spills and Dreams**

With pen in hand, let visions flow,
In every drop of ink, our dreams grow.
The canvas of life awaits our touch,
A masterpiece crafted, we dream so much.

Each stroke of passion, each line of care,
Creates a tapestry beyond compare.
In the silence of night, our thoughts take flight,
Launching us into the infinite light.

Breathe in the stories, let them unfold,
For in each word, a universe bold.
Ink spills over, igniting our soul,
Transforming our fears, making us whole.

As dreams unfurl like wings of a dove,
We find our purpose, and rise above.
So write your truth, let the ink flow free,
For in the world of dreams, we shall be.

With each confession, each heartfelt gleam,
We carve our own paths, we dare to dream.
In ink spills and moments, our spirits sing,
Creating a world where hope takes wing.

## Tangles of Time and Telling

In every twist, a tale unfolds,
Moments woven, truth it holds.
The past and future intertwine,
A journey marked by fate's design.

Paths diverge like rivers wide,
Choices echo, where dreams collide.
Step by step, we carve our lane,
In every joy, in every pain.

Embrace the now, the fleeting hour,
Find strength within, unleash your power.
In tangled dreams, let hope ignite,
A brighter dawn, a guiding light.

Each story shared, a thread we weave,
In every heart, we learn to believe.
For time is endless, vast, and bright,
In every shadow, find the light.

# The Palette of Narrative

Colors splash on canvas wide,
Every hue, a heart's inside.
From reds of passion to blues of calm,
In art's embrace, we find our balm.

Brush strokes dance, a story flows,
Life's vibrant tale, in details shows.
Each moment captured, every sigh,
An endless journey, we fly high.

With every shade, a memory blooms,
In every doubt, a vision looms.
Paint your dreams with fearless grace,
In this vast world, you find your place.

The palette speaks a silent truth,
Of hopes reborn, reclaim your youth.
In every color, life's essence shines,
An artist's heart, where love entwines.

## Silhouette of a Plot

In shadows deep, a story stirs,
Through silent nights, adventure whirs.
Figures dance in twilight's grace,
With every silhouette, find your place.

The whispering winds, a soft embrace,
As dreams take flight, we find our pace.
Through valleys low and mountains high,
A plot unfolds, beneath the sky.

With courage bold, step into light,
Unravel threads, embrace the fight.
Each heartbeat charts a course anew,
In every choice, you'll see what's true.

The canvas waits, let your voice resound,
In every silence, strength is found.
So carve your path, make dreams your own,
In this silhouette, you have grown.

## **Threaded Realities**

In webs of thought, we weave our dreams,
Through tangled lines, the heart redeems.
Each thread a tale, together spun,
In threaded worlds, we are all one.

Bound by visions, we rise and fall,
In every lesson, we hear the call.
A tapestry of hopes and fears,
In every stitch, a world appears.

The loom of life, it spins so grand,
In every knot, a guiding hand.
Unlock the patterns, brave and bright,
In every woven strand, find light.

With every pulse, new realms we blend,
In threaded realities, we transcend.
So take a breath, embrace the flow,
In this grand weave, let your spirit grow.

# Bridging Imaginations

In dreams we find our wings,
Across the skies we soar,
With each new hope that sings,
We open every door.

The bridges built with care,
Connecting hearts and minds,
A tapestry so rare,
In unity, it binds.

A spark ignites the night,
As shadows drift away,
With courage as our light,
We shape a bright new day.

Embrace the unknown quest,
With passion as our guide,
In every heart, the zest,
For dreams that do abide.

Together we will stand,
In harmony we grow,
A world that feels so grand,
With love, our spirits glow.

## The Hidden Paths of Prose

In whispers of the night,
Words dance on paper's stage,
Where feelings take their flight,
And stories break the cage.

With every stroke and line,
We weave a vivid tale,
As souls begin to shine,
In nuances that sail.

The hidden paths we tread,
Unearthed by brave hearts true,
With ink, our dreams are fed,
And visions come to view.

From silence springs a voice,
Emerging from the past,
Inviting us to choice,
Where shadows fade at last.

So turn the page with grace,
Embrace the words you find,
Each prose a hidden place,
To heal the heart and mind.

## **Whispers of Ink**

In the stillness of the night,
Whispers flow from the pen,
With dreams in every flight,
A journey to begin.

Ink spills secrets untold,
In forms both bold and bright,
A canvas wide and bold,
That captures pure delight.

With each word, we can share,
Emotions deep and true,
A silent tender care,
That binds both me and you.

Let stories intertwine,
As pages turn and turn,
In every heart, a sign,
Of wisdom we can learn.

So let your spirits soar,
In verses softly spun,
With ink forever more,
Our legacy's begun.

## Threads of Imagination

In threads that weave and spin,
A tapestry unfolds,
Where fantasies begin,
And every thought enfolds.

We stitch the dreams we crave,
In colors rich and bright,
With courage, bold and brave,
We craft our own delight.

The fabric of the mind,
A canvas deep and wide,
Where every soul can find,
A place to dream and glide.

Let visions intertwine,
Like stars that fill the skies,
With hope, our hearts align,
As boundless as our ties.

So gather up the threads,
And weave with joy and care,
For in each life, it spreads,
An art beyond compare.

## The Dance of Desires

In shadows soft, hopes take flight,
Whispers of dreams in the hush of night.
Each step we take, a spark ignites,
In our hearts, a symphony of lights.

Through tangled paths, our spirits soar,
Hurdles faced, we strive for more.
With every heartbeat, our truth aligns,
The dance of desires, in love, it shines.

Moments weave a tapestry grand,
With courage found in a gentle hand.
Together we'll rise, through trials and fears,
In the rhythm of life, laughter and tears.

Let passion lead and grace unfurl,
As we twirl through the vibrant world.
In unity, we set forth our stance,
Boundless, we'll twine in this sacred dance.

# Celestial Chronicles

Stars whisper secrets in the velvet sky,
In their light, lost dreams learn to fly.
Threads of time, like silver strands,
Weaving our fates with gentle hands.

Planets align with rhythms divine,
Each moment a spark, a reason to shine.
A journey unfolds with every breath,
In the tapestry of life, we conquer death.

Galaxies twirl in a celestial dance,
Inviting our spirits to take a chance.
The heart pulsates with the universe's beat,
In this cosmic waltz, we find our seat.

Echoes of love resonate far and wide,
In the vast expanse, we all abide.
With open hearts, we embrace the night,
Painting our stories with radiant light.

## Storylines of the Soul

In every heartbeat, a tale is spun,
Chapters of life with each rising sun.
Pages unfold with lessons untold,
In the ink of passion, our dreams are bold.

Through valleys low and mountains high,
With every challenge, we learn to fly.
The essence of love cascading bright,
In the storylines of the soul, we ignite.

Each voice a note in the grand parade,
Unity in diversity, a serenade.
Brushstrokes of hope on a canvas vast,
Embracing the future while cherishing the past.

With wisdom gained from joys and scars,
We reach for the heavens, the light of stars.
Together we write, weaving heart and mind,
In this ever-evolving story, we find.

## **Dappled Dreams**

In morning light, dreams softly gleam,
Painted with colors of a waking dream.
Every whisper of wind, a gentle call,
Dappled moments, inviting us all.

Under the shade of the ancient trees,
Hope dances lightly on the breeze.
With every leaf that twirls and sways,
A reminder to cherish our fleeting days.

Sunbeams dappling the forest floor,
Each gleaming fragment, a hidden door.
In the quiet, the heart finds peace,
Allowing all burdens and worries to cease.

So let us wander through this enchanted sphere,
Fill our lives with love and cheer.
As dreams weave gently into the seam,
We awaken the magic in dappled dreams.

## **The Landscape of Lore**

In valleys low, where dreams take flight,
The mountains whisper tales of light.
A river flows through time and space,
Each bend a chance, a new embrace.

The sun arises, painting skies,
Awakening hopes, where courage lies.
With every step, the past ignites,
Transforming fears to soaring sights.

The winds carry songs both old and bright,
In every shadow, there's a guiding light.
Together we rise, with hearts so wide,
In this landscape, let your spirit glide.

Every trail leads to a door,
Unlocking dreams we can't ignore.
With eyes aglow, we chase the dawn,
Embracing magic, pressing on.

So forge ahead, with stories bold,
In each heartbeat, let joy unfold.
In the landscape of lore, be free,
For endless wonders wait, you'll see.

# Parchments of Possibility

Each page we turn, a chance revealed,
With ink of hope our fate is sealed.
The stories start in quiet sighs,
As dreams awaken, truly rise.

On parchment bright, our futures scrawl,
In every word, we stand tall.
Embrace the lines that twist and turn,
In every page, there's much to learn.

Ink flows freely, like a stream,
In every heart, lives a dream.
With every thought, we shape our way,
Finding light in every day.

So write with passion, let love guide,
In this journey, walk with pride.
Parchments await, our stories vast,
In each moment, shadows cast.

With courage bold, let's turn the page,
Embrace the life, and break the cage.
In the book of dreams, we dare to pen,
The tale of now, again, again.

## Serpentine Stories

Through winding paths, our voices flow,
In layers deep, the stories grow.
They twist and turn, yet always seek,
A spark of truth in every peak.

The winds recall the tales of old,
Of battles fought and hearts of gold.
With every breath, a rhythm beats,
In serpentine patterns, life repeats.

Beneath the brush, where legends dwell,
In each soft whisper, stories swell.
Embrace the curves, the twists of fate,
For in every tale, we resonate.

The journey's long, yet oh, so sweet,
With footsteps light, we're bound to meet.
In every fold, a lesson lies,
The magic deep within us flies.

So weave your dreams through every thread,
In serpentine tales, where passions spread.
In stories shared, we all take part,
Together we rise, embraced by heart.

# Horizons of the Heart

In every dawn, a promise glows,
The horizon calls, where passion flows.
With arms outstretched, we greet the day,
In search of joy, come what may.

The skies above paint dreams in hue,
In every shade, life feels anew.
The road ahead is wide and bright,
Guided by love, we chase the light.

As stars ignite the night so clear,
Our hearts align, casting aside fear.
In every whisper, hope takes flight,
Together we soar, boundless in height.

So step forth boldly, with heart aglow,
In horizons vast, we learn and grow.
With faith as our anchor, we set sail,
In the seas of life, we shall not fail.

With every heartbeat, let's explore,
The beauty found in love's great lore.
In horizons of the heart, we stand,
Together, we'll dream, hand in hand.

# Beneath the Surface of Words

In whispers soft, the truth does lie,
Beneath the surface, dreams take flight.
With courage found in silent sighs,
We navigate the depths of night.

Each sentence carved with care and grace,
A bridge across the vast unknown.
In every pause, we find our place,
A spark of hope that we have sown.

The heart speaks loud when silence reigns,
In every letter, light is stirred.
Through trials faced and endless pains,
We seek the beauty found in words.

So let us dive into the sea,
Where language flows like gentle streams.
With open minds, we learn to be
The architects of all our dreams.

For in the quiet of the night,
The stories twine like threads of gold.
Beneath the surface, pure delight,
Awakens worlds waiting to unfold.

# The Odyssey of Thought

Imagine worlds beyond the shore,
Where thoughts can sail and dreams take wing.
With every step, we long for more,
An odyssey the mind can bring.

Through valleys deep and peaks so high,
The journey shapes our very soul.
We chart the paths that make us fly,
In search of truths that make us whole.

With every challenge, we discover,
A spark that lights the darkest night.
Our hearts unite, we help each other,
Together we embrace the fight.

So let the winds of change be strong,
And guide us through the tempest's roar.
In unity, we all belong,
Each thought a wave upon the shore.

An odyssey, a dance, a song,
Where every voice a treasure found.
We journey forth, we all belong,
For in our minds, the world is crowned.

## **Illuminated by Inspiration**

In shadows cast, a light does gleam,
An ember flickers, bold and bright.
With every thought, we chase the dream,
Illuminated by the night.

Each moment holds the spark of grace,
An idea waiting to take flight.
With open hearts, we find our place,
In every mind, a star ignites.

Through trials faced and mountains climbed,
Inspiration flows like rivers free.
We weave the threads of hopes entwined,
Creating art for all to see.

So let us paint the skies with words,
Let colors blend and visions burst.
In every voice, a song is heard,
A symphony of dreams immersed.

For in the light of every soul,
A fire burns to guide the way.
Together we can reach our goal,
Transformed by inspiration's sway.

## **The Tapestry of Tales**

In every thread, a story spun,
A tapestry of life displayed.
Through laughter shared and battles won,
The tales of hope will never fade.

Each hue represents a voice,
A life that danced with joy and sorrow.
In woven dreams, we find our choice,
To shape a brighter, new tomorrow.

The fabric rich with love and pain,
Each pattern echoes bold and true.
Through every joy and deep disdain,
The stories link me and you.

So gather round and share the lore,
For in our words, we build a home.
Together, we can dream of more,
And through our tales, we shall not roam.

In this vast quilt of time and space,
We find our belonging, intertwined.
The tapestry of tales we trace,
Our legacies forever signed.

## The Untamed Narrative

In the wild where dreams take flight,
Stories whisper through the night.
Each heart beats a tale untold,
A vibrant canvas, brave and bold.

With every step, the path unfolds,
New horizons, bright and gold.
Embrace the twists, the turns, the bends,
For in each struggle, the spirit mends.

Let courage soar like wings of light,
Break the chains that bind your sight.
The untamed leaps, the fearless roam,
In every heart, the quest for home.

In unseen realms, find your voice,
In silent echoes, make your choice.
Paint your passion on the sky,
With every heartbeat, dare to fly.

The tale is yours, let it ignite,
From shadows deep, emerge to bright.
Write your legacy, page by page,
The world awaits your boundless stage.

## Stars in a Script

In the night, the stars take stage,
Words like constellations engage.
Each thought a twinkle, bold and clear,
A cosmic dance, a story near.

Let your hopes be the guiding light,
Inspire dreams, chase the night.
With every line, a spark ignites,
A universe of endless sights.

Scripted journeys in skies so vast,
Whispers of futures, shadows cast.
Every heartbeat, a poem's spark,
Shine like the stars, defy the dark.

With ink and courage, draw your fate,
From every triumph, elevate.
In the stars, your story sings,
Awake the magic that dreaming brings.

Let go of fears, let visions soar,
In every word, find so much more.
Write with passion, let courage grip,
The cosmos echoes your soaring script.

## Evolution of Echoes

Each sound a ripple, a journey wide,
Echoes of wisdom, time as a guide.
In the silence, the heart will learn,
Transformation in every turn.

From whispers soft to thunderous roars,
The past holds keys to open doors.
Seek the lessons in the air,
Embrace the whispers everywhere.

As echoes evolve, let hope arise,
Beneath these shadows, clarity lies.
Every heartache, a stepping stone,
In the dance of life, we are not alone.

Listen closely to the stories spun,
The journey begins, the race is run.
In every note, a chance to grow,
Evolution of echoes, let it flow.

With every breath, embrace the change,
From simple lessons to the strange.
We are the echoes of tales yet told,
In the grand design, be brave and bold.

## **The Journey of the Jotted**

With pen in hand, the dreams ignite,
Thoughts take shape in the soft moonlight.
Each stroke a step, a path to tread,
The journey lies where the heart is led.

From scribbles small to visions grand,
The future waits, just take a stand.
In letters woven, hope is spun,
The journey swells, it's just begun.

In every draft, a flicker glows,
The heart pours out, the spirit flows.
Through every word, let passion blaze,
Illuminate the silent ways.

With every page, the story grows,
The ink's embrace, the dreamer knows.
Courage found in every line,
The journey blooms, your dreams align.

So fill the pages, don't delay,
The journey of the jotted, pave the way.
In each creation, a world unfolds,
Your path of dreams, in essence, bold.

## Murmurs of the Mundane

In the quiet dawn's embrace,
We find whispers of our dreams,
Each moment tells a story,
In simple, subtle themes.

The rustle of the leaves above,
A reminder to believe,
In every thread of daily life,
A chance for joy to weave.

Each step upon the winding road,
Is painted bright with hope,
In the mundane's gentle grip,
We learn to stretch and cope.

The laughter shared, the fleeting gaze,
In small things, magic hides,
Illuminate your every path,
With love that gently guides.

So pause and breathe the air anew,
In each day's tender light,
For every whisper speaks to you,
That you, too, can take flight.

## The Weaving of Wonders

Threads of color intertwine,
In a tapestry so bright,
Each moment's spark ignites the heart,
Filling the world with light.

Hand in hand, we craft our dreams,
With hope as our guiding star,
In the fabric of existence,
We stitch the near and far.

Every laugh, a vibrant hue,
Every tear, a silver thread,
Together we create a world,
Where love and courage spread.

In the loom of human touch,
A pattern starts to show,
With each connection that we make,
A beautiful flow.

So gather all your wishes close,
And dare to dream once more,
For in this grand design of life,
We open every door.

## The Canvas of What If

Upon the canvas of our minds,
Thoughts dance like vibrant paint,
With every stroke, a question grows,
In colors bold and faint.

What if the sky were filled with dreams,
Soaring on winds of chance?
What if our hearts could echo light,
In every joyful glance?

With every 'what if' whispered soft,
New worlds begin to form,
In the imagination's realm,
Creativity is born.

So let your heart explore the space,
Where possibilities reside,
In every brush of hope and love,
Our passions will collide.

Awake the dreams that call to you,
Embrace the bold unknown,
For every canvas tells the tale,
Of seeds we've all sown.

## Layers of Luminescence

Beneath the surface, light resides,
In layers rich and deep,
Each story glows with wisdom's shine,
In shadows, secrets keep.

The heart is like a precious gem,
With facets yet unseen,
When polished by our trials strong,
It sparkles, fierce and keen.

In every challenge that we face,
A lesson waits in guise,
Like dawn that breaks the darkest night,
Revealing the sunrise.

So peel away the doubts we hold,
And let the light break free,
For in each layer of our being,
The truth is meant to be.

Embrace the journey of the soul,
As you uncover grace,
For in every ounce of struggle,
There lies your radiant space.

## **Journeys Beyond Boundaries**

Across the horizon, dreams ignite,
Steps unfurl in morning light.
With every pulse, the world expands,
Adventures lie in distant lands.

Hearts take flight on winds of change,
Embracing paths that feel so strange.
Through valleys deep and mountains tall,
We rise together, never fall.

Opportunities, like stars, align,
In every soul, a spark divine.
Boundless trails await our hearts,
In unity, the journey starts.

Believe in whispers of the heart,
Each new venture, a brand new start.
With courage lighting up the way,
We chase our dreams, come what may.

So gather strength, embrace the ride,
In every heartbeat, hope resides.
Journeys shared, our spirits bright,
Together we can touch the light.

# The Manuscript of Memory

In the book of life, pages unfold,
Stories written in whispers bold.
Ink of laughter and tears we share,
Crafting moments beyond compare.

Every chapter, a lesson learned,
Through shadows deep, our spirits burned.
Embrace the past, with wisdom gain,
Seek the joy in every pain.

Footprints linger in golden sands,
Echoes of time in gentle hands.
Memories bloom like flowers rare,
A tapestry beyond compare.

With every heartbeat, life imparts,
A symphony of countless hearts.
Memories guide us through the night,
Illuminating paths with light.

So pen your tale, let courage swell,
In every line, a truth to tell.
The manuscript writes of love's embrace,
In the journey, find your place.

## Surreal Sketches

In a canvas woven with dreams and grace,
Artistry reflects a tender space.
Colors swirl in a dance of light,
Creating worlds both strange and bright.

Each brushstroke tells a story untold,
Whispers of magic for hearts to behold.
Imagination paints realms unknown,
In surreal visions, we find our home.

Clouds of wonder drift through the skies,
Mirrors of life through uncharted eyes.
Dreams awaken, a canvas anew,
In every heartbeat, art rings true.

Let the brush guide your heart's refrain,
In the interplay of joy and pain.
In every image, a journey spins,
Unlocking the treasure that life begins.

So sketch your dreams, let colors flow,
In the realm of the inner glow.
Surreal sketches, forever embrace,
The beauty of time, a sacred space.

## **Tidal Waves of Imagination**

In waves that crash upon the shore,
Imagination opens every door.
With each tide, fresh ideas rise,
Washing over the skies we prize.

Like seashells scattered on golden sand,
Thoughts emerge, surreal and grand.
Creativity flows with each refrain,
A symphonic dance, joy and pain.

Ride the currents, feel the embrace,
Harness the power of this vast space.
Let visions soar on the crest of dreams,
In the depths, find shining beams.

When imagination lifts the veil,
Boundaries fade; together we sail.
In the ocean of thoughts, we navigate,
Finding treasures that hearts create.

So dive deep into the endless sea,
Tidal waves of wild esprit.
In every ripple, a spark ignites,
Infinite dreams in boundless flights.

# Weaving Dreams in Ink

In ink, we weave our dreams so bright,
Each word a star that twinkles light.
With hope as our guide, we craft the tale,
A ship to sail where hearts prevail.

The pages turn, a dance of grace,
In every line, we find our place.
Through trials faced and lessons learned,
With ink and passion, our fires burned.

A tapestry of thoughts unfurled,
In every story, a new world.
So pen your dreams, let courage soar,
The ink is magic, forevermore.

With every stroke, new hopes arise,
A fearless plunge into the skies.
We gather strength from what we write,
In dreams of ink, we find our light.

## Tales from the Writer's Forge

In the writer's forge, with heated thoughts,
We mold our tales, all fears forgot.
Each character shaped with love and care,
In fires of passion, we lay them bare.

With hammers of hope and anvil of dreams,
We craft our stories, ignite their beams.
Every challenge faced, a lesson learned,
From steel to words, our souls are turned.

Ink flows like metal, strong and pure,
In every tale, our hearts endure.
So take the leap, embrace the spark,
For in that forge, we leave our mark.

The stories weave through time and space,
In every line, a warm embrace.
So share your gifts, let your voice be heard,
From the writer's forge, each thought's a bird.

## The Alchemy of Imagination

In the cauldron of thought, ideas swirl,
Transforming dreams in a vibrant whirl.
With every spark, new worlds ignite,
In the alchemy of night, we find our light.

Gold from words shaped with care,
A potion brewed, beyond compare.
Each letter a gem, in darkness they gleam,
We conjure visions, a timeless dream.

With quill as wand, we cast our spells,
Creating magic, where wonder dwells.
A landscape rich, where thoughts run free,
In this alchemy, we cease to be.

So lift your voice, let creation flow,
In imagination's grasp, we learn to grow.
Through every story, we find our path,
In the alchemy of dreams, feel the warmth and laugh.

## Whispers of Unwritten Stories

In quiet corners, stories sigh,
Their whispers dance beneath the sky.
With every thought, a tale awaits,
In unformed dreams, the heart creates.

They linger soft, like morning mist,
The unwritten words, we can't dismiss.
So take a breath, and listen close,
In every silence, new worlds can grow.

The echoes call, with gentle might,
Inviting us to share their light.
With open hearts, we weave the thread,
Of tales untold, and words unsaid.

Each whisper holds a spark divine,
In every pause, a chance to shine.
So let them flow, unbound, set free,
For in these stories, we find our we.

## Secrets Beneath the Surface

Beneath the calm, the waters flow,
Whispers of dreams where courage grows.
Hidden gems in depths so vast,
Unveiling truths from shadows cast.

Dive deep within, uncharted seas,
Find strength in silence, set your mind free.
Every wave, a tale to tell,
Secrets dance where spirits dwell.

With every heartbeat, listen close,
In quiet moments, find your dose.
The surface shimmers, but don't be fooled,
Real treasures lie where hearts have cooled.

In every ripple, in every sigh,
Lies the essence of how to fly.
Trust the journey, embrace the call,
For hidden wonders await us all.

So take a breath, and dive right in,
Let the waves of life begin.
With each descent, your spirit climbs,
Discovering joy in unknown times.

## **The Quixotic Quest**

Upon the dawn, dreams take their flight,
A noble heart seeks the distant light.
With every step, a story unfolds,
Woven in courage, timeless and bold.

Mountains high and valleys low,
Embrace the journey, let your spirit glow.
In every challenge, a chance to grow,
The path may twist, but hope's the flow.

Chasing visions, wild and free,
With laughter guiding, just let it be.
From hills of doubt to skies of grace,
Every moment adds to the chase.

Fathomless dreams in a world so wide,
Through storms and calm, let love be your guide.

For every struggle, a lesson learned,
In the quixotic quest, hearts are burned.

So rise each day with purpose bright,
Let inner flames be your alight.
To seek the impossible is a noble feat,
With passion as fuel, the world is your seat.

## Whims of the Wordsmith

In shadows cast, the words take flight,
Crafted in whispers, woven in light.
With ink and quill, the soul speaks clear,
Creating worlds that draw us near.

Each phrase a brushstroke, vivid, bold,
Painting emotions that never grow old.
Through stanzas rich, and verses profound,
In written magic, the heart is found.

A tapestry spun with care and delight,
Where dreams are born in the dead of night.
In every line, a piece of the heart,
Reminding us all that we're never apart.

From sonnets sweet to tales of woe,
The wordsmith's whim allows love to flow.
So dance with the letters, let passion rise,
For in their embrace, a future lies.

With every syllable, a spark ignites,
Illuminating paths on darkest nights.
So write your truth, let the stories merge,
In the whims of the wordsmith, let hearts surge.

## **Embracing the Unsaid**

In silence rests a treasure rare,
Where feelings dwell, beyond compare.
A glance, a smile, the unvoiced song,
In the stillness, we truly belong.

Words may falter when hearts collide,
But deep connections cannot hide.
Embrace the pauses, the weight of a sigh,
In unsaid moments, spirits fly.

For what is spoken can fade away,
But the heart's soft murmur is here to stay.
In quiet understanding, we find our peace,
A shared existence that will never cease.

Let the shadows of doubt be shed,
With love's bright light, no words need be said.
In the unsaid lies the truest grace,
Together, we uncover a sacred space.

So celebrate the whispers, the unspoken truth,
For in quiet moments, we reclaim our youth.
With each heartbeat, our souls align,
Embracing the unsaid, oh, how we shine.

## The Mounting of Metaphors

In the cradle of dawn's embrace,
Dreams take flight, a gentle race.
Mountains rise in whispered grace,
Echoes of hope, a sacred space.

Words unfurl like petals bright,
Casting shadows, chasing light.
Each thought a star, burning white,
Guiding hearts through the night.

In every struggle, seeds are sown,
In trials faced, true strength is grown.
With every climb, new strength is known,
From valleys deep, we find our own.

Metaphors dance, in unity twirl,
Transforming pain in gentle whirl.
They lift us up, like sails unfurl,
Together we rise, as one, we swirl.

A tapestry woven in vibrant threads,
A mosaic of stories that life spreads.
In every heartbeat, a message treads,
A reminder that hope never sheds.

## Colors in the Silence

In quiet corners, colors bloom,
They paint the walls, dispel the gloom.
Silence whispers in shades of plume,
Each hue a promise, a sweet perfume.

In shadows deep, ideas ignite,
In stillness found, we grasp the light.
Every moment, a canvas bright,
Waiting for dreams to take their flight.

Soft blues cradle the tender heart,
And golden hues pull us to start.
With every stroke, a brand new part,
Colors intertwined, a work of art.

Through the silence, our spirits sing,
A symphony of everything.
In quiet depths, we find the spring,
A vibrant life that hope can bring.

As colors merge, our fears release,
In the calm, we find our peace.
With every shade, we learn to fleece,
The burdens fade, and joy increase.

## The Elixir of Expression

Words flow like rivers, deep and wide,
A channel for truths we cannot hide.
In every verse, our souls confide,
The elixir of life, where dreams abide.

Each thought a droplet, glistening clear,
Gathering strength, casting out fear.
In the art of expressing, we draw near,
To the essence of love that we hold dear.

In the dance of language, we find our way,
Through whispered tales and bright display.
Fragments of joy in what we say,
A potion brewed to seize the day.

Let passion flow in every line,
With every heartbeat, the stars align.
In the journey of words, we brightly shine,
Crafting legacies, uniquely divine.

So lift your voice, let it be known,
In the gift of expression, we're never alone.
Our stories entwined, forever shown,
An elixir of spirit, brightly grown.

# Timeless Tales

In the pages of time, stories unfold,
Whispers of wisdom, shimmering gold.
Each tale a treasure, waiting to be told,
Moments captured, forever bold.

From shadows cast, the heroes rise,
With dreams as wings, they touch the skies.
In every chapter, hope never dies,
A spark ignites, as hearts revise.

In laughter shared and tears that flow,
A tapestry rich, with highs and lows.
Timeless tales where love still grows,
In every heart, the flame bestows.

Let voices echo through the ages,
Inspiring words in all their stages.
Each story breathes, as time engages,
A legacy forged, turning pages.

As night descends, and stars alight,
In every tale, we find our might.
Together united in endless flight,
Timeless tales, our guiding light.

## Chasing the Quill

With every stroke, a story grows,
Ink on the page, as the passion flows.
Dreams take flight in the quiet night,
Chasing the quill, igniting the light.

Whispers of hope dance in the air,
Unfolding tales with gentle care.
A world awaits beyond the ink,
Through every line, we start to think.

The heart encourages the mind to soar,
With every word, we long for more.
A journey penned, where courage sings,
Inspiration blooms on papered wings.

Beyond the horizon, visions expand,
Embrace the dreams; take a stand.
For every quill holds a thread of fate,
In the tapestry of life, we create.

So let the ink flow, let the dream chase,
In the chase of the quill, we find our place.
With each new page, we rise anew,
Chasing the quill, in all that we do.

## Scripting the Unknown

In shadows deep, the words take flight,
Scripting the unknown in the dimmest light.
With courage forged, and hearts ablaze,
We pen our dreams through the darkest days.

As pathways twist and futures blend,
Every word crafted, a tale to send.
Beyond the fear, beyond the doubt,
In our stories, the truth breaks out.

A script unfolds in the quiet space,
Where dreams collide and fears erase.
With every line, we learn to stand,
Creating a world that's grand and planned.

In uncertain realms, we find our way,
Through every challenge, we choose to stay.
A journey penned, with strength conferred,
Scripting the unknown, we speak our word.

So grasp the pen, embrace the quest,
In every struggle, find your rest.
For in the unknown, we find our song,
Scripting the unknown, where we belong.

## Chronicles Born of Dreams

In softest whispers, a chronicle starts,
Born from the dreams woven in our hearts.
Each tale untold, a treasure revealed,
Unlocking the strength that's eternally sealed.

With every heartbeat, the stories thrive,
Fueling our spirits, keeping dreams alive.
In pages turned, we find our way,
Chronicles echo what words can't say.

A tapestry woven of hope and grace,
In the dance of time, we find our place.
For every dream is a chapter new,
In chronicles born, our spirits accrue.

Together we rise, united in thought,
In the quest for meaning, lessons are taught.
With every line written, we gather strength,
Chronicles born, we journey at length.

So let your dreams flow into the light,
For in every story, there lies our might.
From dreams to words, let your heart gleam,
Chronicling all that we dare to dream.

## Visions in Vellum

Upon the vellum, visions awake,
Crafted in silence, our souls partake.
With colors bright, and shadows cast,
In this sacred space, our thoughts hold fast.

Whispers of futures dance on the page,
Every ink-stroke, a tiny sage.
Through trials faced, we learn to see,
Visions in vellum, where we can be free.

A canvas awaits the brush of dreams,
In hues of hope, the spirit gleams.
With each rising dawn, our hearts explore,
Visions in vellum, forevermore.

Together we sketch, both brave and bold,
Every narrative a truth to hold.
In every detail, our passions blend,
Visions in vellum, where dreams transcend.

So take the time to breathe and create,
In the art of life, we celebrate.
For in our visions, the world aligns,
Visions in vellum, our dreams define.

## Layers of Language

In whispers soft, the words arise,
Layered dreams beneath the skies.
Each syllable a path revealed,
A tapestry of truth concealed.

Voices echo through the years,
Carving hopes, dispelling fears.
With every phrase that we define,
A chance to grow, a chance to shine.

In every tongue, a story lives,
An art of giving, love that gives.
With every note, the heart ignites,
In gentle tones, the soul takes flight.

So let us speak, let dreams unfold,
In vibrant hues, both brave and bold.
Together weaving words divine,
In layers deep, our spirits twine.

## Fragments of Forgotten Lore

In shadows dance the tales of old,
Fragments glimmer, stories told.
Each whisper carries ancient grace,
Reviving life in time and space.

Through musty tomes and crumbling pages,
Winds of wisdom through the ages.
A spark ignites the embered mind,
Resurrecting what we left behind.

With every line, a chance to learn,
In echoes past, our spirits yearn.
For lore forgotten, hearts reclaim,
The fire of knowledge, our eternal flame.

So seek the shards, let visions soar,
In fragments found, we seek much more.
For through the past, a way we find,
To weave our futures, intertwined.

## The Storyteller's Palette

With brush in hand, the tales unfold,
Colors bright, emotions bold.
Each stroke a heartbeat, fresh and wise,
Crafting worlds beneath the skies.

In shadows' depth and light's embrace,
The storyteller finds their place.
Through laughter, tears, raw and true,
A canvas paints the life anew.

Every shade holds dreams untold,
The vibrant tales that we behold.
In artful hues, our hearts collide,
On this grand journey, side by side.

So let us weave our stories bright,
In every color, pure and light.
Together in this vibrant dance,
The storyteller leads the chance.

## **Scripting Fantasia**

In realms of dreams, our visions play,
Scripting fantasies in a dazzling array.
Each word a star, a spark of might,
Igniting worlds with pure delight.

Through ink and quill, adventures rise,
Imagination's gift, a grand surprise.
We wander paths of endless grace,
In every line, a warm embrace.

So pen your dreams, let spirits soar,
For every tale opens a door.
In vibrant hues and wild design,
The magic lives, the scene is thine.

With hands outstretched, the canvas waits,
To script the life that destiny creates.
In every tale, we find our way,
Scripting dreams, come what may.

## **Venturing Beyond the Margins**

Step forth into the unknown light,
Each whisper of hope ignites the night.
Embrace the journey, hold it tight,
The future unfolds, a wondrous sight.

With open hearts, we'll chase the dreams,
Breaking through barriers, or so it seems.
In every shadow, a glimmer beams,
Together, united, we'll build the themes.

Oh, venture wide, let courage swell,
Beyond the edges where stories dwell.
In every challenge, let passion tell,
The strength in us, an enduring spell.

So leap into paths where hearts align,
Find your truth in each twisting line.
With every step, life's colors shine,
Embracing the journey, it's yours and mine.

In the arms of the brave, we'll find our song,
With voices rising, we'll all belong.
Together we'll wander, forever strong,
Venturing beyond, where dreams prolong.

## **Verse Brews Beneath the Stars**

Under the dome of infinite night,
Whispers of wishes twinkle with light.
Dreams brewed with care in the heart's delight,
Stirred by the cosmos, shining so bright.

In laughter shared, constellations form,
Stories unraveled through every storm.
With every heartbeat, the magic's warm,
Together we rise, our spirits transform.

So gather 'round, let the verses flow,
In shadows and light, our dreams will grow.
With eyes on the sky, our hearts aglow,
Beneath the stars, life's moments bestow.

Crafting our tales as the night flies by,
Each word a spark, igniting the sky.
In rhythm, we find the reasons why,
Verse brews beneath, with dreams that won't die.

In harmony found, we'll dance and sing,
With every line, let the universe ring.
In the vast expanse, our hopes take wing,
Verse brews beneath, a wondrous thing.

## The Canvas of Experience

Life paints whispers in vivid hues,
Each stroke is a tale, each color imbues.
Through trials and triumphs, we learn to choose,
In the canvas of life, there's nothing to lose.

Beneath every brushstroke, lessons await,
In moments of silence, we contemplate.
Through laughter and heartache, we cultivate,
An artful existence, it's never too late.

So gather your colors, don't hold them back,
In splashes of joy, let your spirit unpack.
With passion and purpose, shape your own track,

The canvas of life calls—no need to act.

Embrace every moment, let creativity soar,
From every sunrise, to every uproar.
Crafting experiences we can't ignore,
A masterpiece born from living and more.

In the gallery of time, our stories live on,
Each brush brings us closer, our fears overthrown.

In the canvas of experience, together we've grown,
A vibrant mosaic, forever our own.

## Sonnet of Whimsical Journeys

In dreams we wander, so bright and clear,
Through valleys of laughter, over hills of grace.
With footsteps of joy, we move without fear,
Embracing each moment, our hearts interlace.

A tapestry woven with threads of delight,
In every adventure, our spirits take flight.
From dawn's gentle glow to the moon's silver light,
Whimsical journeys, forever ignite.

With imaginations free, we'll soar ever high,
Across boundless skies where visions align.
Embodying wonder, like stars up on high,
Each story we tell, an art so divine.

Through twists and turns, we'll remember these days,
In the sonnet of life, we'll dance and we'll play.
With smiles and laughter, we'll color the ways,
Whimsical journeys, unfolding our ways.

So come take my hand, let's wander anew,
Through fields of enchantment, where dreams will accrue.
In this sonnet of journeys, it's me and it's you,
Together we'll weave a world bright and true.

# Threads of Thought

In whispers soft, ideas bloom,
A tapestry of visions loom.
Each strand a pathway, bright and clear,
We weave our dreams without fear.

With every step, the world unfolds,
A canvas rich, with tales untold.
Embrace the light, let shadows cease,
Find clarity, and seek your peace.

Through winding roads, we journey on,
With strength anew, like dawn's first song.
United hearts can break the mold,
Each thought a thread, a story bold.

Let courage rise, let spirits soar,
In unity, we find the core.
With open minds, we pave the way,
To brighter paths, to a new day.

In every thought, a spark ignites,
Together, we reach new heights.
Threads of hope that intertwine,
In the fabric of the divine.

## Mosaic of Mind's Eye

In fragments bright, the colors blend,
A world created, no end to tend.
Each piece distinct, yet part of whole,
A dance of dreams that fills the soul.

With every glance, a vision grows,
Inpatterns vast, the spirit flows.
We paint our truths, each stroke a sign,
Of journeys marked, and hearts aligned.

Through trials faced, we learn and rise,
With every tear, we touch the skies.
In unity, our stories merge,
Together, we ignite the surge.

With gentle hands, we craft the light,
In darkest hours, we spark the fight.
A mosaic rich, in hues so bold,
Tales of love and hope retold.

Embrace the dreams that call your name,
In each arrangement, find the flame.
A vision vast, a heart so free,
In our mosaic, all can see.

## Ink Rivers and Paper Skies

With every word, a river flows,
In ink so deep, the story grows.
The paper skies, a soft embrace,
In dreams reflected, we find our place.

With whispered thoughts upon the breeze,
We capture moments, hearts at ease.
With every line, a pathway carved,
In this adventure, we are starved.

A quill that dances, sparks ignite,
Bow to the muse, embrace the light.
From shadows cast, the tales emerge,
In ink rivers, our spirits surge.

With moonlit nights, our secrets spill,
On paper skies, we find our thrill.
A tapestry of words we weave,
In every verse, we believe.

Let stories flow, let knowledge soar,
In this vast sea, there's always more.
Ink rivers rich, and skies so wide,
In every heart, let truth abide.

## The Fabric of Fables

In stories told, we find our ties,
The fabric woven under skies.
With threads of hope, and dreams so bright,
We spin our fables, day and night.

In tales of old, in legends grand,
We grasp the strength, we take a stand.
Each fable sparks a fire within,
A journey shared, where all begin.

With every page, a lesson learned,
In chapters rich, our passions burned.
Through laughter shared and sorrows bared,
The fabric glows, a love declared.

Embrace the tales that shape our fate,
In every word, we elevate.
Together stitched, a vibrant thread,
With every fable, hope is spread.

Let echoes linger, let voices rise,
In stories told beneath the skies.
The fabric of fables, strong and free,
In every heart, our legacy.

## Chasing Shadows on Blank Pages

In the quiet dawn, I find my muse,
Whispers of dreams that I can choose.
Each word a spark, lighting my way,
Guiding my heart through the soft gray.

With courage I pen, I let ideas flow,
Chasing shadows, where hopes gently grow.
Each line a journey, a path to tread,
Unfolding stories yet to be said.

The blank page beckons, a canvas so wide,
In its silence, my thoughts can confide.
Embrace the unknown, and dare to create,
For within these lines, I shape my fate.

With every stroke, I craft a new tale,
A symphony of voices, a vibrant sail.
Through valleys of doubt, I'll rise and fight,
For every shadow reveals a new light.

So here I stand, with pen in my hand,
Ready to weave the dreams that I planned.
In chasing shadows, I'll find my song,
In the pages of life, where I belong.

# The Art of Wordsmithery

Crafting my thoughts with care and grace,
Each phrase a reflection, a moment in space.
Words intertwine like a delicate thread,
Weaving the magic of things left unsaid.

In the realm of ink, I build my tower,
With every verse, I discover new power.
The rhythm and cadence, they dance and sway,
Inviting the heart to join in the play.

Sculpting my visions in metaphor's light,
Each stanza a dance, an exquisite flight.
Through laughter and tears, my spirit ignites,
In the art of wordsmithery, the soul takes flight.

With open arms, I embrace the unknown,
A tapestry woven, the seeds I have sown.
The beauty of language, a treasure to hold,
In the craft of creation, a story unfolds.

Here lies the power, in letters and rhyme,
An echo of voices, transcending time.
In every creation, a piece of me lives,
In the art of wordsmithery, my heart gives.

# Sketching Realities in Rhyme

With pencil in hand, I sketch my thoughts,
Drawing the dreams that time has forgot.
Each line defines the world I see,
In the canvas of life, I'm finally free.

The colors of emotion bloom in the air,
A symphony painted with passion and care.
Rhyme becomes the brush, my feelings ignite,
Sketching the beauty in the depths of night.

From shadows to sunshine, I trace every hue,
Creating a vision that's honest and true.
The stories awakened beneath my own hand,
Sketching realities, in this vibrant land.

Each stanza a moment, each verse a glance,
Inviting the heart to join in the dance.
With every creation, a piece of my soul,
In sketching realities, I feel more whole.

The world comes alive through my artful embrace,
Each rhythm a heartbeat, each image a grace.
In this tapestry woven, my spirit finds rhyme,
Sketching realities, transcending all time.

## Echoes of Silent Epics

In the hush of the night, stories whisper low,
Echoes of epics in the moon's gentle glow.
With each heartbeat, the past comes alive,
In the silence, our tales begin to thrive.

Each hero and villain, a dance in the dark,
Their struggles and triumphs ignite a spark.
In chapters unseen, our dreams intertwine,
Echoes of silent epics, a journey divine.

As time weaves its tapestry, moments unfold,
With courage and passion, our stories are told.
In whispers, we listen, our hearts open wide,
To the echoes of life that no one can hide.

Through valleys of silence, the ancients still call,
With lessons of wisdom that rise and that fall.
In the stillness, we gather, we carry the weight,
Of echoes of silent epics, it's never too late.

So stand on the precipice, breath in the air,
Embrace all the stories for we all have a share.
In the echo of time, let our voices take flight,
For in the realm of silence, we spark the light.

Milton Keynes UK
Ingram Content Group UK Ltd.
UKHW021402081224
452111UK00007B/125